from

PTSD

— *to* —

PTG

Other Books by
DR. DAVID GRIFFIN

ACTION:
9 Missions for Personal and Professional Growth

In Honor of The Charleston 9:
A Study of Change Following Tragedy

from
PTSD
to
PTG

A Firefighter's (My) Journey
After a Multiple LODD Incident

DR. DAVID GRIFFIN

Paperback:
ISBN 10: 0-692-88282-0
ISBN 13: 978-0-692-88282-5

This book represents the author's research and does not represent the views of his employer in the fire service. This is solely his work. Furthermore, ideas presented in this book are not to be viewed as a medical diagnosis or recommended treatments for mental health conditions. This is a memoir of how one person overcame PTSD in hopes it will inspire others to do the same. Names, genders, ages, and identification may have been changed for confidentiality purposes.

10 9 8 7 6 5 4 3 2 1

It's go time. . .

For those who are lost.
I hope this helps you find your way. . . .

Table of Contents

Foreword

By: Melissa Griffin

You may have heard of the tragic furniture store fire in Charleston, South Carolina on June 18th, 2007. Well, I'm here to introduce you to the journey of the driver of the first due engine on that fateful day. My husband, my best friend. . . David Griffin. I'm honored to give you a brief glimpse of David's journey, and in turn, our journey as well.

This voyage began with days and even years of overwhelming silence, rage and depression following the incident. It was heart wrenching to say the very least. David turned to alcohol, pain killers, uppers, downers, a pink Mohawk and sleeve tattoos. Who was I to say how he should deal with his guilt? His anger? His emotions?

David was absolutely lost and I, in turn, was lost too. I couldn't even begin to imagine what was going on inside his mind, his heart, his soul, his being. I still can't.

During this time, we were just approaching our one year wedding anniversary, and we were competing together, David within NPC (National Physique Committee) bodybuilding and myself NPC then IFBB (International Federation of BodyBuilders) figure. After the incident, it didn't take long for David to turn elsewhere, specifically mixed martial arts (MMA). It was his "out," so to speak. And trust me, when he sets his mind to something, he goes 1000% all in, and nothing—I mean nothing—will get in his way.

Now let me give you a little history here. David played shortstop for The Citadel, The Military College of South Carolina. During his senior year, he was hit directly in the face with a fastball while going in for a bunt. David's face was shattered, eye socket broken, and emergency surgery ensued. Against all odds, David came back and won the opportunity to play professional baseball in the Independent Frontier League. From there, David's next athletic endeavor was bodybuilding (as previously mentioned) where he was crowned overall state champion in 2006. Next up, MMA, which we will get back to momentarily. Then IRONMAN triathlons.

Author's Note

On Tuesday June 19, 2007, I was relieved on the scene of a multiple line of duty death incident (LODD) in Charleston, SC around 7:30 am. Since 7:11 pm the night before, I was the pump operator of a fire engine as nine firefighters perished in a furniture store. The scene was an absolute disaster. Much of the 42,000-square foot commercial structure collapsed. The air smelled of burnt wood, plastics, chemicals, and sweat. I was covered in dirt, soot, and stench. I had been awake for 27 hours. I was tired, I smelled as if I hadn't showered in days, and I wasn't processing what I just experienced. Adrenaline kept me going all night as we continued to fight the fire and the recovery crews removed the nine firefighters. I saw things that night I wish my mind could forget.

When it was time to leave the scene, I grabbed my contaminated gear, which was worn by an off-duty firefighter, and put it in my red 2005 GMC pickup truck to make my way home to my wife. I pulled onto Savannah Highway, the road directly in front of the furniture store, and was surrounded by national news outlets, police officers, people holding signs, and basically hysteria. People were screaming and crying as they tried to get closer to the scene of the incident. I was not ready for that.

I tried to drive away from the collapsed building, but I was overcome with emotion. As I saw the chaos around me, my mind couldn't process it. It felt as if the world was flying by me at an intense speed. Everything seemed so fast, blurry, and confusing. I immediately started having flashbacks of what I just experienced. My heart started racing, my hands started shaking, I was sweating immensely, and I began to cry. I continued to drive for about 500 yards until I pulled off the side of the road. I sat in my truck while cars flew by me. I was crying, shaking, and trying to figure out what the hell was wrong with me. I had never felt like this before. The emotional state of my mind was consuming my body to the point where I didn't think I could drive home.

I sat there for about 10 minutes attempting to calm myself down. I saw a police officer in the street to my left directing traffic. He saw me having a difficult time but there was nothing he could do. He didn't know who I was or what I was experiencing at that moment. He continued to direct the speeding cars as I struggled to collect myself. I just couldn't do it though. My heart continued to race, now my entire body was shaking, my brow was covered in sweat, and I was crying hysterically. I felt like such a weak person because I couldn't control what was happening to me. After all the training from The Citadel on mental toughness, I figured I could beat anything. This time I was wrong. This was the start of a journey that would take me to places I never imagined. Over the next decade, I would go to the lowest of lows, pick myself up repeatedly, and finally reach the point where I could help other people from my experiences.

Let me be very clear on this point. This is not a badge of honor for me. I do not like talking about Post-Traumatic Stress Disorder (PTSD) or the incident where nine great firefighters perished. I also don't enjoy being away from my family for over 175 days a year while I travel with a message that requires me to relive a traumatic event repeatedly. This is not fun for me. I do not get jollies off the work I do. However, I do it because I've chosen a path of Posttraumatic Growth (PTG) to deal with my inner turmoil and hopefully, to save people's lives.

Does everyone agree with it? No, and that's all right. I respect their opinion, but at the end of the day, I must do the work I've been called to do. I didn't plan for this to be my life's work, but now that it is, I will give it all I have. I don't know any other way to move forward.

As Mark Twain stated, "The two most important days in your life are the day you are born and the day you find out why." I was born on September 5, 1980. It took me 27 years to find out why. Unfortunately, it came after a traumatic incident that I pray every day didn't occur. The problem is I had to spiral through darkness to find the light I needed to regain control over my life. It's my hope this book will help you find the light you're looking for. I'm not an expert and I don't profess to be one. I'm just a man who has a unique skill set due to my experience with a multiple LODD incident, PTSD, and now the education to help others. I cannot and will not go to my grave with the knowledge I've gained without passing it on to others. I have a responsibility now bigger than me. The Mission continues. . . .

—Griff

CHAPTER

I

What is PTSD?

Post-Traumatic Stress Disorder (PTSD) is a mental health condition some individuals develop after they witness or experience a life-threatening or terrifying event. This is a common issue affecting more than three million individuals in the United States yearly. It's a treatable disorder that can be resolved by medical professionals. However, with emergency responders continual experience with traumatic events, it's much more difficult to combat the symptoms. Why? Because some of us witness trauma repeatedly for decades. Constant exposure to traumatic events doesn't allow for healing to occur. If proper professional help isn't utilized, PTSD can develop and cause mental health challenges in one's life to the point where they can no longer work. According to the United States Department of Veterans Affairs National Center for PTSD, there are four types of symptoms of PTSD:

1. Reliving the event:

   • Nightmares, constant thoughts, memories, and flashbacks of the incident.

2. Avoidance of certain situations that present reminders of the event:

   • This can include people, situations, specific locations, and even the avoidance of talking about the trauma.

3. Continual negative feelings:

   • Survivors guilt may present itself where you feel numb, shameful, or guilty.

WHAT IS PTSD?

- Loss of interest in activities that once were enjoyable.

4. Hyperarousal:

- Always on edge, anxious, nervous, and looking out for dangerous situations.

- Mood swings that present anger, irritability, and unhealthy living.

- Easily startled.

While the above described symptoms are important, individuals suffering from PTSD may also experience alcohol abuse, drug abuse–prescription and/or street drugs, physical ailments, difficulties with employment, interpersonal relationship problems, and trust issues. We must remember, PTSD can impact anyone. It just doesn't occur in soldiers and emergency responders. It impacts all types of people at all levels of society. What may seem traumatic or stressful to you, may not seem that way to another person and vice versa.

There are many different factors that impact how an individual will respond to trauma. However, there are a

13

few specific factors whether an individual will develop PTSD. They include:

- Previous traumatic experiences.

- Age.

- Gender.

Notice, *previous traumatic experiences* was number one on that list. Hence, the reason emergency responders have a higher rate of developing PTSD. We see trauma repeatedly. This is not healthy.

Firefighters are now being studied in relation to PTSD due to their continual exposure to traumatic incidents. According to Dr. Matthew Tull, individuals who have experienced "multiple traumatic events have been found to be at a greater risk for developing PTSD." These multiple traumatic events can include medical emergencies, motor vehicle accidents, rescues, suicides, dead on arrival, structure fires, shootings, stabbings, rapes, murders, and a host of other incidents we experience. How do these responses impact the percentage of firefighters with PTSD? Well, Dr. Tull indicates anywhere between 7% and 37% of firefighters "meet criteria for a current diagnosis of PTSD." That's alarming.

Professional help must be obtained by individuals suffering from PTSD to ensure lifelong mental health problems don't ensue. In the emergency services world, this hasn't always been accepted. Many of us were told to suck it up and not let the job bother us. Well, that advice hasn't worked out too well. Some people have sucked it up for so long one day they decide to end it all. So, if you're still giving that advice because you think you're tougher than everyone else, please stop. You're hurting other emergency responders who need help.

Sadly enough, many emergency responders are suffering from PTSD and either don't know where to go for help or are embarrassed to ask for help. How do we fix this problem? First, education regarding mental health and PTSD should be provided to our employees continually. Second, we must also provide our employees with proper programs they can utilize during times of traumatic stress. We can't wait for a traumatic event to occur and then decide to create a mental health plan. This plan needs to be in place as a proactive step to minimize PTSD, mental health issues, and suicide. Third, we must continually monitor our employees for PTSD signs and symptoms and be bold enough to help them. We can no longer just let people figure it out on their own. This is a dangerous practice and can end up having deadly consequences.

Finally, we must educate our employees on the concept of Posttraumatic Growth (PTG). Yes, we will continue to experience traumatic events in our line of work. However, if we utilize our proactive steps of education, mental health programming, continual monitoring, and education on the concept of PTG, we can assist our co-workers in combatting the effects of PTSD. Let's teach them how to turn a negative into a positive and grow from the incidents that have plagued their psyche. If we can do this, noticeable changes will occur. How do I know this? Because all of what you just read on PTSD is what I experienced. However, with PTG, I was able to overcome my issues. It can do the same for you if you will give it a chance, stay positive, and believe in yourself. Your journey From PTSD to PTG, begins now. . . .

2

What is PTG?

PTG, Posttraumatic Growth, is a phenomenon where an individual grows stronger and develops more meaning in their lives following a traumatic experience or tragedy. This concept was developed in 1995 by Dr. Richard Tedeschi and Dr. Lawrence Calhoun, professors of psychology at the University of North Carolina at Charlotte. They interviewed more than 600 victims of traumatic events and found many of them believed their lives had improved following the tragedy in specific areas at different periods of time. Why? Because they processed what they experienced and made foundational changes in how they lived.

This doesn't just relate to military personnel, fire-fighters, emergency medical technicians, and police officers. It can relate to civilians who experience trauma as well. Take Candace Lightner for example. In May of 1980, her 13-year-old daughter Cari was walking home from a carnival when she was hit by a drunk driver and killed. Her mother was absolutely devastated. What did she do? She went to Capitol Hill and made a speech that would develop a movement called MADD, Mothers Against Drunk Driving. Some sources state she's saved over 600,000 lives over the last 35 years. Yes, she was involved in a devastating tragedy that took her little girl from her, but she didn't let it beat her. She took the road less traveled, faced her pain, and did something to ensure it didn't happen again. I can guarantee you it's not easy for her to do the work she does. However, she has the motivation and conviction to do it. Why? Because one of her twin daughters was killed by a drunk driver. What better person to develop a program to reduce drunk driving by ensuring stiff punishment for the offenders? NO ONE. She is the best person for her Mission. Search for her online and watch her interviews. She is focused, pre-cise, and dead set on her Mission. She is not in the media because she wants to be. She is in the media because she has to be; for her daughter.

Another example is former NFL football player Steve Gleason. This man lives to the fullest. Watch his movie titled "Gleason" and you'll see what I mean. As a linebacker at Washington State, he was extremely fast and aggressive. He was a smaller player but no one could deny his ability to put a strong hit on an opponent. From the college and NFL videos I've seen of him, he had two speeds: fast and faster. He was an incredible athlete where his abilities earned him an opportunity to play in the NFL. He will be forever known for the punt he blocked on September 25th, 2006 in the New Orleans Saints first game in the Superdome after Hurricane Katrina. It resulted in a touchdown on the same play. There's a statue of his block in front of the stadium. It was incredible to see.

Three years after retiring in 2008 from a nine-year career in the NFL, he was having some strange medical issues. Muscles were twitching in his arms, shoulders, chest, back, and legs. He sought out medical professionals to ascertain why. In 2011, he was diagnosed with ALS, Amyotrophic Lateral Sclerosis, often known as Lou Gehrig's disease. According to the ALS Association, this is a progressive neurodegenerative disease that affects nerve cells in the spinal cord as well as the brain. This leads to a gradual degeneration and death of motor neurons which causes people to lose the ability to move, speak, eat, and even breath. It has no cure as of this book's publication date.

When he was diagnosed with ALS, he set out On A Mission to make a video for his unborn child. The disease progresses quickly so he wanted to ensure he could teach his son before becoming wheelchair bound. While I watched his movie, which is a documentary he recorded from before his battle with ALS began, all the way until he can no longer talk or do anything for himself, I was brought to tears. Yes, he was having a difficult time mentally and physically with his disease. You could see it in his emotions and movements. However, as he physically regressed, he reached a point where he became mentally stronger. He went on to create The Gleason Initiative Foundation and The Gleason Family Trust to raise money for others who suffer from ALS and to allow himself to participate in experimental treatments. His hope is to help others through this disease with better technology, medical care, and ultimately, to find a cure.

Since its inception, his foundation has raised millions of dollars and helped thousands of people around the world. He is actively involved in the foundation and wants to continue to help others. Did he have to do this? No. He could've given up a long time ago. But he didn't, even though he unfortunately experiences the mental and physical pain of ALS every day. He combined this experience with an in-depth knowledge of the disease and how he could make life more comfortable for others suffering from it. His diagnosis with ALS changed not only his life, but countless other lives. What better person to be an advocate for individuals suffering from ALS than Steve Gleason? NO ONE. We must understand there is a plan for all of us in life. That plan may not always be what we dreamed of or expected. However, it is our responsibility to make the best out of it. We do this by sharing experiences with others to allow growth. Steve Gleason is a perfect example of PTG. He will never quit and I'm a better person for learning from him. It made me realize what's important.

Another example of PTG is John Walsh, a man who's been hunting criminals for over 30 years as a television host. He's been the host for numerous criminal hunting programs including the most notable, Americas Most Wanted. This wasn't his original plan, though. He lived a great life in Florida as a hotel developer with his wife and son. Then in 1981, his son was kidnapped from their home at the age of six. Two weeks after the abduction, his son's severed head was found 120 miles away in a canal. From this tragic incident, John made it his Mission to locate criminals so they could be prosecuted. According to the FBI, John's television program, Americas Most Wanted, led to 17 captured fugitives who were once on their top 10 most wanted list. Other research indicates over 1200 suspected criminals were captured due to the show.

John also went on to create a national database for missing children by motivating Congress to pass the Missing Children Act, which then led to the development of the National Center for Missing and Exploited Children. Since 1984, more than 196,000 missing children were found due to John's creation. He accomplished all of this and saved hundreds of thousands of lives because his son was kidnapped and beheaded. Do you think he wants to make a living like this? I would say no. However, he does this work because he has the passion to save missing children. It's pretty apparent why. Who better than to be on this Mission? NO ONE. When he searches for a criminal, he's driven by his son and the love he has for him. That's what makes his work so special. He took a negative incident and turned it into a positive outcome for hundreds of thousands of people. That's Posttraumatic Growth.

CHAPTER
3

Processed the Incident

Processing the incident on June 18, 2007 was challenging for me. I had such insignificant knowledge and experience in the fire service then and really wasn't aware of what I just went through. I read an article in our hometown newspaper stating our firefighting tactics were too bold and outdated. When I read this, I became angry because I was proud of our department and its rich history. I thought everyone else was fighting fire incorrectly and they should be operating the way we did. I was unaware of many of the technical terms being used in the media and the equipment they exclaimed we should've had.

An outside panel of investigators were hired to travel to Charleston to assess the department and the operations used on June 18, 2007. When I heard these "Northerners," yes, I just said that, were coming to Charleston to research us, my sentiment was they had no idea why we fought fire the way we did. That shows you my ignorance.

These "Northerners" included firefighters with 100+ years of experience and education collectively. The leader was Gordon Routley, followed by Michael Chiaramonte, Brian Crawford, Peter Piringer, Kevin Roche, and Timothy Sendelbech. These are all well-educated, dynamic leaders who knew the progressive fire service. But I had no idea who they were then. I asked myself, "Why should they perform the study?" Well, outside individuals needed to perform the evaluation to ensure a fair and unbiased report. I didn't understand this then. Obviously now, I do.

When the panel arrived, I gave them the cold shoulder every chance I could. When they asked to interview me for their report I was standoffish and protective because it felt as if I was being interrogated. Uh, I was, and rightfully so. They were trying to piece together a puzzle more complex than they ever imagined.

After months of interviews and research, the first

phase of *The Routley Report* was published in October of 2007, followed by the second phase in May of 2008. I didn't know what to expect when I read the report. When I finally did, I was overwhelmingly shocked with the information included. There were terms I never heard of, equipment I didn't know existed in the fire service, operations of a commercial structure fire I was unaware of, radio procedures I never educated myself on, and scientific information about the products burning inside the building.

Specifically, when I read the first finding, "The situation that occurred in Charleston on June 18, 2007 was predictable and the outcome was preventable," I was even more angry because at first I didn't agree with that. However, as I continued to read, I became upset with myself because I didn't know or understand what the panel's findings meant. This is when I began to process the incident. Why? Because I started to read other information about the tactics and technologies available during 2007. I was so upset I didn't educate myself previously to know them. I don't blame other people for my lack of knowledge in the fire service then. I blame myself. I should've attended classes, conferences, read trade magazines, and understood the reasons for why we do what we do in the fire service. Unfortunately, I did not.

Have you ever heard of the saying, "You don't know what you don't know"? How about this one, "You don't know what you don't know, until you don't know—then it may be too late"? Thanks to my friend John M. Buckman III for sharing that one with me. It's true though. You don't want to find out you don't have sufficient knowledge or experience on an emergency scene. That should be done in training.

I continued to read *The Routley Report*, as well as *The National Institute for Occupational Safety and Health (NIOSH) Report*, and *The National Institute for Standards and Technology (NIST) Study*. I was repeatedly left shaken by what I read. I realized I didn't have the necessary level of mastery needed in my profession. What do I mean by this? According to Lieutenant Colonel Dave Grossman in his best-selling book titled, *On Combat*, there are four levels of mastery. The first level of mastery is unconscious incompetence. Unconscious incompetence basically means you don't know what you don't know. You don't possess the ability to process a situation because either you've never been in that particular situation before or don't have education for it. This is when we have the unfortunate opportunity to make decisions based on our ego rather than a RPDM, recognition-primed decision-making.

Recognition-primed decision-making refers to our

minds ability to recall information from knowledge or experience and apply it in a current decision-making process. This is essential in making educated decisions in emergency situations. Well, when you're at a level of unconscious incompetence, you don't know, that you don't know, that you're not operating with best practices. I was unconsciously incompetent. If I would've learned more, better educated decisions were possible. Realizing that you're unconsciously incompetent is a major step of processing where you are and where you need to be.

The second level of mastery is called conscious incompetence. Now you know, that you don't know. So, what do you do? You must educate yourself by taking college courses, fire service classes, leadership programs, and hands-on training to bring yourself up to the third level, conscious competence. This means you can now perform a new skill, but you must think about it in-depth. This level of mastery is sufficient during training because that's when you're learning. However, conscious competence isn't necessarily sufficient for operations on an emergency scene. We must train to the fourth level of mastery; unconscious competence. This indicates you've practiced a skill so much, you can perform at a high level in a stressful environment. We must all strive to attain this. We must also remember when we reach the level of unconscious competence, continual learning is necessary. Why? Because if new tactics are developed and we rely on the fact we have unconscious competence with the old tactics, we are now in a possible new level of mastery no one wants to talk about; complacency.

Human behavior research indicates when we develop certain levels of competence, we go on auto pilot too much, which can create a dangerous environment. Just because we're good at a skill doesn't mean we should skip thinking about it. We must still process the current incident to make the right decision based on the modern environment, not the way we've always done it.

Learning the four levels of mastery allowed me to process the multiple LODD incident I experienced. I was impressed by what these levels taught me about my lack of knowledge, skills, and abilities as a young fire-fighter. It opened my eyes to the fact I needed to train extremely hard on tactical skills as well as educate myself on the science behind fire. When you understand why you're doing what you're doing, you'll be much better at whatever task that may be. Processing information correctly allows you to do so. Once you can objectively process the information, it's time to develop a plan for improvement. The problem for me was I didn't know where to start. What classes did I need? What was I lacking? Therefore, I turned to someone I once hated and now looked up to as a mentor. It was time to ask for direction from someone who could assist me in developing a plan for progress.

CHAPTER

4

Developed A Plan

I was unsure of how to overcome all the disrespect I directed to our new command staff from 2008-2011. I needed direction and a plan for not only professional improvement, but personal improvement as well. I set out to let go of my past beliefs of the new leaders so I could start fresh. You see, when our new Fire Chief, Thomas Carr, arrived in Charleston in 2008, I wasn't happy because we hired someone from the outside. Then I heard he was from the north. Yes, I just said that again. Another testament of my ignorance at that time.

Over the next year, Chief Carr developed plans for our organization starting from scratch. When I found out he was making all of the monumental changes, I was livid. Again, ignorance on my part. How embarrassing.

Chief Thomas Carr was a highly-respected leader in the fire service who was previously the Chief of Montgomery County Fire and Rescue Services in Montgomery County, Maryland. During his tenure there, he successfully brought multiple departments together, with over 1,000 firefighters, to operate in a countywide system. That's an incredible feat. He accomplished this because of his incredible leadership capabilities, in-depth knowledge of organizational change, and political know how. He was amazing once I stopped being ignorant and allowed myself to learn from him. I watched him at city council meetings, in the stations, on the news, and in public. This made me realize the type of leader he was; a servant leader. This was the first servant leader I worked with so I was eager to learn more about the principle.

Servant leadership is defined by Robert Greenleaf as a philosophy or set of practices that enriches the lives of individuals, constructs better organizations, and creates a more caring and just world. If we think about that definition, it relates to our profession of public service. To fully understand the concept, we must discuss the

10 specific characteristics of a servant leader. They are as follows:

- **Listening**: As leaders we must listen intently to what others are attempting to communicate to us, both verbal and non-verbal. This means put down the cell phone, stop typing on the computer, and give your full attention.

- **Empathy**: Understand other people's needs and accept them for their uniqueness. Look to the positive of other individuals work, even if you must reject their ideas or performance.

- **Healing**: Remember, you can heal others by healing yourself. This is essential for not only personal transformation, but also organizational progress.

- **Awareness**: One must have self-awareness and foster that in other individuals.

- **Persuasion**: The utilization of persuasion rather than rank in making decisions, i.e. convince members of the importance of a decision rather than coercing compliance.

- **Conceptualization**: See the big picture rather than just day-to-day operations. Dream big.

- **Foresight**: Remember past lessons, present realities, and the repercussions of current and future decisions.

- **Stewardship**: Every individual in an organization has the responsibility in holding members and the organization accountable.

- **Commitment to the Growth of People**: The value of an organizational member goes beyond them just being an employee. Ensure they grow at all levels including personal, professional, and spiritual.

- **Building community**: Determine areas the organization can foster community relationships, community involvement, and community progression.

Chief Carr embodied these principles with his

actions every day. It was amazing to watch his magic. At first, I didn't buy it because I thought it was a gimmick. However, I quickly realized this man was a truthful, genuine, and caring individual who focused on how he could make us better with every move he made. He had a gift.

This was around the time I was attempting to accept Chief Carr, but I was still struggling with it. One day in particular, he arrived at the station in the afternoon. He was dressed in civilian clothes and accompanied by his wife. I was exercising at the time, running 400-yard shuttle runs combined with muscle-ups. I remember this because I ran by him while he was in front of the station talking to the other firefighters. As I sprinted by with my sleeved tattoos and pink Mohawk, I gave him the best mean mug I could offer. I did this every time I passed by. He just looked at me and smiled. I said to myself, "Why is he smiling? There's nothing funny going on here." When I finished the 400-yard run, I jumped up on the pull-up bar to knock out muscle-ups. Suddenly, he walked up to speak with me with that same smile on his face. He shook my hand sternly and spoke very artic- ulate. Obviously, I didn't intimidate him at all. That was my first lesson from him in leadership. He was kind and professional to me no matter how I had treated him since his arrival in 2008.

Well, over the next year we crossed paths but I didn't like him at all. He was making historical changes to our organization I didn't agree with. When he developed certain items, I laughed at them and said, "Good luck with that." Yes, I said that because I was a disrespectful and ignorant person then. I was so confused about how to feel about the fire service and what I was going through, I just lashed out at the leaders. This is not an excuse; it's the truth. This man was developing new policies and procedures while I was doing anything I could to buck the system because I thought it would make me cool. The problem is people around me were buying into the system and I wasn't. I brought a tremendous amount of negativity on my co-workers at that time. This is not who I was raised to be. I was raised to be positive, disciplined, and most importantly, respectful. I graduated from an historical military institution, The Citadel, but unfortunately, after 2007, I turned into a joke. I was unable to control my emotions or be a good follower for my leaders. Finally, the time to change arrived. I had to put my hatred down so I could turn to leaders who could help me. Low and behold, I turned to the man I hated for two years, Chief Carr. Via email, I asked him for a meeting regarding career development. He probably read that email and thought I lost my mind. I knew I had to start new with him but I didn't know if he would give me a chance. As I entered the meeting in my fire department uniform, I was extremely nervous because I didn't know how he was going to act towards me. I had disrespected him for two years. He stuck his hand out to shake mine, was very professional, and acted as if nothing ever happened. I was blown away. I thought he was going to hold a grudge against me; but he didn't. I truly believe he understood I was having a difficult time emotionally with the fire and the monumental number of changes.

When the meeting began, I was preoccupied with the easel pad paper he had spread all over the walls of his office. He had different titles on the pieces of paper. For example, apparatus, raises, grants, training, Incident Command, and a host of other topics. I was in total disbelief when I saw this. This man was On A Mission.

I started to ask him questions about how I could educate myself to the level I needed to be in the fire service. He suggested a plan for me which included fire service classes like Fire Instructor I and II, Fire Officer I and II, the National Fire Academy leadership series, Incident Safety Officer, Fire and Life Safety Educator, and many more. He also explained I needed to perform hands-on training every shift to bring my skills up to a higher level. This conversation went on for over an hour. He answered all my questions and helped me develop a plan for improvement. I needed this plan to pull me out of the hole I dug for myself emotionally. It allowed me to get on the right track in our profession, but more importantly, it taught me valuable life lessons.

You see, I never met this man before 2008 but I judged him as a leader before I gave him a chance. Shame on me. I totally disrespected someone who was trying to save my life both personally and professionally. He was performing his job with the utmost professionalism and leading by example. This man taught me the error of my ways, shaped how I make decisions today, and impacted how I carry myself. I will never be able to thank him enough for helping me develop a plan to save my life.

So how does this relate to you? Well, a plan gives you direction and something positive to focus on rather than dwelling on the negative. When the negative is focused upon, nothing good will be accomplished. It also makes it difficult for you to be a good follower. Remember, if you aspire to be a leader, you must first be a good follower. I assure you if you're negative and spread your discontent around an organization, it will be difficult for you to be a good follower. Why can I say that? Because that was me. I was the one spreading hate and discontent while others were trying to make progress. Without a plan, I would've remained lost. Without someone willing to assist me with that plan, I wouldn't be where I am today. The plan was another measure that saved my life from PTSD and allowed me to grow. A positive plan can do the same for you.

CHAPTER
5

Talked with A Professional

Historically in the emergency services field, a person is viewed as weak if he or she says a certain call or series of calls bothers them. After all, we're supposed to be invincible, mentally and physically, right? Well, if you still feel this way, you're sadly mistaken. When we begin the profession of helping others, we see many sad incidents throughout our years. Yes, it's a part of the job. However, if we think we can store these sad incidents somewhere deep in our mind and forget, we're causing a great deal of mental anguish on ourselves. We all have different ways of dealing with traumatic emergency scenes so I'm not going to tell you how you should deal with them. What I'm going to do is tell you how I dealt with them not only after June 18, 2007, but even before this incident because I was scared to show others that some emergency responses bothered me.

The first call signifying an emotional connection for me was only a few days into my career in 2005. I had only been through a 6-week course called *1152*, which in South Carolina is a basic introduction to structural fire-fighting, and a 9-day recruit school before I was riding an engine as a firefighter. I didn't have any EMS training for the first few weeks I was on the engine because I was awaiting the first responder class.

During one of my first shifts, the engine I was detailed to received a call for a full arrest. Even without any EMS training, I knew what that meant. My heart started racing because I had never seen anyone having a heart attack or knew what to do. I jumped on the rig as we sped down a small one-way street. I remember walking into the home to see the hysterical family members. Right off the bat I was having a difficult time focusing. We walked to the second floor where the family members were screaming their loved one was. I stormed into the cluttered room and didn't see anything that resembled a person. I scanned the bed and the floor but I still didn't see anyone. Suddenly, as I scanned the bed again, I noticed a small shape of a person who was as white as the bedsheet. It took a few seconds to register but when it did, I realized that was the patient. The patient was blending in with the white sheets. I immediately felt an emotional connection because I wasn't prepared for what I saw. That was the first dead body I was ever exposed too. I didn't understand what I was witnessing.

When the EMT's arrived, I walked downstairs and jumped back on the engine. As we were riding back to the station, I couldn't get the sight of the patient out of my head. I felt so bad for the family. You could tell they cared for their loved one so much. In that moment, all I could think about was my family and how much I loved them.

When we arrived back at the station, I watched to see if the call bothered the other two firefighters on the rig. They both possessed many years of experience and responded to that type of emergency plenty of times. They had their own way of dealing with it by then. I was just learning. I was afraid to ask anyone if they felt like I did after the first time they saw a dead body. I didn't want my co-workers to think I was soft or mentally weak.

So, what did I do? I walked upstairs like nothing

bothered me. I immediately grabbed my shower gear so I could clean up before bed. When I closed the bathroom door at the station, an overwhelming feeling of sadness for that family came over me. I shook if off at first but when I was in the shower, it hit me like a ton of bricks. I starting sobbing, then crying. All I could think about was how sad that family was and how much I loved my family. I stood in the shower for about 20 minutes clearing my head and coming to grips with what I just saw. I finally collected myself, finished the shower, and tiptoed to bed for the remainder of the shift. As I laid in my creaky bed staring at the tongue and groove ceiling of a 118-year-old firehouse, I realized this is just as much a mental job as it is a physical one.

Now let's fast forward from that call in 2005 to the days, months, and years following June 18, 2007. Talking to a professional about the incident and how it made me feel didn't even occur to me. I was trying to uphold that tough bravado image of a firefighter. Nothing bothered me, right? Wrong.

I began to hear many people involved in the incident were going to speak with professionals. I didn't want to participate nor did I believe in it at that time. I thought I could deal with the stress by shoving it in the back of my mind. When I saw a newspaper article on the incident or the department, I ignored it. When the news would report on the incident, I would change the channel or get up and leave. When other firefighters talked about it, I would go somewhere else. I didn't want to keep hearing about it because it was bringing back those intense emotions and physical reactions. I would start sweating, my heart would start racing, my hands would shake intensely, and my mind would go back to that day in 2007. I hated those feelings so the only way I knew to cope with them was to cram them away in my mind. I didn't realize I was doing more damage mentally to myself.

Shortly after we hired our new Fire Chief, Thomas Carr, he suggested that many of us speak with mental health professionals about our experience with a multiple LODD incident. Right off the rip, firefighters took this advice to heart. Many were speaking of the great help it awarded them. I was skeptical at first because I didn't think a person sitting behind a desk could even begin to understand what we were experiencing. Well, I figured I had nothing to lose so I decided to give a mental health professional a try.

I arrived for my first appointment so nervous I had cotton mouth. This surprised me. I previously played professional baseball in front of 30,000 plus people, stood on stage as a bodybuilder in front of thousands, and fought an

Ultimate Fighting Championship (UFC) fighter. Those are the activities that gave me cotton mouth. I couldn't believe going to talk to someone who sat behind a desk could do this to me. I told myself I needed to suck it up and stop being soft. Ego and bravado at its best.

Was I just supposed to walk in a room and talk to someone I didn't even know or trust? That seemed impossible to me. As soon as I saw the counselor, I said to myself, "This lady has no idea what I'm going through. This is a total waste of time." Even with this thought beating in my head like a jackhammer, I put a smile on my face, shook her hand, and introduced myself. As soon as I sat down, I wanted to get up and walk out. Fortunately, I was already at the point of no return, so I took a long deep breath and let it play out.

The counselor was trying to inspire me to talk about why I was there. At first, I didn't want to participate. I just sat back in my chair acting uninterested. She asked me a few questions and I just disregarded them. I wasn't letting this lady get in my head. I was a tough firefighter. Nothing bothered me. Then as she continued to talk over the next 10 minutes, I sensed that she knew what she was doing. I sat up in the chair and started to focus on what she was saying. It was as if a light bulb went off in my head. What she explained to me struck a chord. So, I decided to give her a chance.

When I first starting talking, it was just a few short sentences. I still didn't trust this process, but I was trying. I finally started to tell her about my anger, fear, frustration, emptiness, sleeplessness, anxiety, nervousness, agitation, and disappointment with myself for feeling so weak. I was embarrassed to be saying this because I always had the utmost confidence in myself. At this point, I had none. I was really struggling. I left the office unsure if I would return.

Over the next few days following the meeting, I replayed the session in my mind. I realized even with the small amount of information I told her, I felt somewhat relieved to have it off my chest and out of my head. I figured what else do I have to lose. So, I decided to return.

Over the next few sessions the counselor wanted to utilize a procedure called EMDR, Eye Movement Desensitization and Reprocessing Therapy. This is a "psychotherapy treatment that was originally designed to alleviate the distress associated with traumatic memories." Researchers believe EMDR "therapy facilitates the accessing and processing of traumatic memories and other adverse life experiences to bring these to an adaptive resolution." During the treatment, "the client attends to emotionally disturbing material in brief sequential doses while simultaneously focusing on an external stimulus," such as therapist directed lateral eye movement (EMDR Institute, Inc.).

When the counselor hinted she wanted to try this on me, I laughed at her aloud. I said, "There's no way I'm falling for that fake treatment." I joked about it for a few minutes as she continued to explain the process and the benefits I would experience. She was very serious and didn't find my laughter appropriate. I could tell she meant business. When I noticed this change in her demeanor, I immediately stopped laughing and began to listen intently. She started to describe other individuals in other parts of the world who utilized this treatment after traumatic events in their lives. She explained FDNY (Fire Department of New York) firefighters used this after 9/11. Once she said that, I was all in. If it worked for those firefighters who lost so many on that horrific day in 2001, it had to work for me.

As I went through the process the first time, I could definitely feel a difference. Not a huge difference, but still a change. I continued this treatment each session and felt myself getting mentally stronger. I was getting my confidence back, my personality back, and I was starting to sleep a little better. I also began to read about EMDR and other ways to overcome stress. This is when I was introduced to stress inoculation.

Stress inoculation comes from the clinical side and consists of three phases to assist individuals with overcoming traumatic events. The first phase is called conceptualization. This is an education phase allowing the patient to assess the problem. I couldn't read the newspaper, watch the news, or hear others talk about June 18, 2007. This was a problem that needed to be dealt with because it was affecting my work, my family, my relationships, my sleep patterns, and my mental capacity. I had identified the problem. Now, I had to fix it.

The second phase of stress inoculation is called skill acquisition and rehearsal. During this phase, the patient targets the problem to develop coping skills. For example, I made myself read the newspaper articles I once ignored. Thanks to my mom and dad, I had all the articles from the local newspaper following the incident. They saved them for me in hopes I could process my experience one day.

When I first started reading them, a tingling sensation surged throughout my body. My hands were shaking again. Anger, frustration, and sadness flooded through my veins. Tears began to flow, but I kept going. I made it through the first article and moved to the next. Same feeling. Then another. Same feeling. Then another.

Hmmm, it was getting better. Then another. No tears this time, just anger and frustration. Then another. Hands stopped shaking and I was breathing normally. I continued this for weeks until I read every newspaper and magazine article I could find on the incident. During this same time, I was watching the news reports online. Those were extremely tough to view because I saw people I cared about saddened and mentally struggling. I continued to push through the news reports and started to join the discussions about the incident with others. I stopped shying away from people asking me questions too. Even though it hurt to talk about, I knew it needed to be discussed so others could learn. I successfully made it through phase two.

Next came phase three, which is application and follow-through. During this phase, the patient focuses on the activities which allow them to transfer coping skills to real life. In doing this, the patient is working to prevent relapse. In relation to my struggle, I couldn't just rely on the fact I read all the reports, newspaper articles, and magazine articles on the incident or I had talked about it a few times. I had to continue to apply my coping skills each time the feeling arose. This was the most important phase for me because I could've easily quit this phase early. Why? Because it was possible I allowed complacency to set in due the progress I made. I knew I wasn't feeling 100% better because the emotions continued to creep back at times. I had to keep applying my coping skills until they became a part of my daily activities. This would keep me mentally strong and allow me to continually evolve my mental health.

I also had to utilize stress inoculation when triggers arose that brought me back to June 18, 2007. Triggers can be defined as smells, sounds, sights, and feelings experienced from a traumatic event. They can quickly bring back the connection to the event causing physical and emotional responses including increased heart rate, tension in the muscles, and intense sweating. I learned about triggers firsthand after the event, even though I had no idea what they were at the time. The main trigger for me was a certain sound in the background of the radio traffic on June 18, 2007. It's hard to explain what it sounds like but anytime I heard it after the incident, it would bring me directly back to standing in front of the pump panel on that day.

On one occasion, I was the driver/operator on another engine about 3-4 months following the incident in 2007. We were responding to an alarm at a 5,000-square foot residential home in an affluent area. The crew went to investigate the alarm while I remained at the engine in case anything was needed. I was standing at the pump panel listening to the radio traffic when a neighbor walked up to me to see what was going on. I explained to him the alarm was going off and we were investigating the source. He then expressed his concern because he believed the home owners were out of town. I figured this information should be passed on to the officer. So, I grabbed my walkie to make a transmission. Before I could, another message came over the radio from another emergency response. Boom, the background noise was there and it set off a trigger inside me. I immediately went back to that day in 2007. So much, I was saying the engine number from June 18, 2007 rather than the engine number I was currently on. I kept calling the officer repeatedly but I didn't get a response. I was worried because I called him so many times. Finally, I realized I was calling the wrong engine number. I couldn't believe the trigger the small background noise had on me. I literally forgot what engine I was on and was saying the wrong resource number continuously.

This was an area I worked hard to overcome in the years following the multiple LODD incident. What did I do to fix this problem? I listened to every minute of the radio traffic from June 18, 2007 to build up a tolerance to the specific sound that triggered my memory. It was difficult the first time because all the emotions came back to me very quickly and were extremely intense. I stopped the radio traffic from playing multiple times, became angry at myself that I didn't keep going, then I'd start it again. I'd listen to it for a few more minutes, then stop it again to calm my breathing down and reduce my heartrate. Then again, and again, and again, and again until I was drenched in sweat, exhausted, my eyes hurt from crying, and my mind was spinning. I did it again the next day. Then the next day, and another day, and the following day, until I could recite some of the radio traffic. It was allowing me to process it and learn at the same time. I was hearing transmissions I never heard before. I realized by pushing myself to listen to the radio traffic, I could help others understand it and learn from it. This was the only way I knew how to beat it. I'm not saying this will work for you or I recommend it. I'm just telling you what I did in hopes something resonates with you.

During this time, I was still going through EMDR treatment as well. From the growth I obtained from both treatments, I had an epiphany one day to research the incident and the organizational progress following it, both positive and negative, at the doctoral level. This intense education phase gave me purpose in life to help others with my same affliction. It also gave me new direction, focus, and the passion to be On A Mission. You will read more on this in Chapter 10.

I'm so grateful I had the opportunity to talk to a professional not only about how the incident on June 18, 2007 impacted me, but also the thousands of other calls I responded to. Many times, it may not be one specific incident that affects us. It's the multiple other responses we go on and store in the back of our minds. We continue to lock them away without purging them by talking to a professional. We do this for years and then one day a call overflows that storage bank and we're overcome with emotion. If we can talk to professionals throughout our career, this will allow us to continue to purge these feelings.

We always train on firefighting, ladders, ropes, EMS, and a host of other tactics but when is the last time we drilled on mental health? Does your recruit program have a mental health class so new members have coping skills before they even get on the rig? Does your developmental program for drivers, officers, chiefs, etc. include a mental health portion? We need to maintain our mental health just as much as we do our physical skills. If we don't, eventually our physical skills will fail us because we'll have a mental block we can't overcome. This could be deadly for an individual and for a crew.

I know we all think we're tough firefighters and nothing bothers us, but that's not the case. It's ok to talk about an incident or a career full of incidents that bother you. If we continue to store these memories, they could erupt one day into a volcano of emotion we can't control. This happened to me more than once and was devastating. I didn't have the guts to admit I needed help. Once I did admit it and talked to a professional, it allowed me to develop coping skills I utilize to this day. It can do the same for you if you will just give it a chance. Trust me, I live it every day and it works. It doesn't make you a weak person to ask for help. It makes you stronger because you had the courage to take your life back.

CHAPTER
6

Substances Were Not the Answer

It all started innocently for me in 2009. I went to the doctor to inquire about why my back was hurting. It was bothering me for a few months but like I did my entire life when I suffered an injury, I ignored it and hoped my body would heal itself. This time was different. I couldn't pinpoint the exact moment when it starting hurting, but I do remember it was the day after I had a high-rise call where I was loaded down with well over 150 lbs. of equipment. I didn't think much of it at first but when it continued to nag me, I thought I should go to the doctor.

Upon examination, the doctor ordered me to undergo a battery of tests and also prescribed pain medication and muscle relaxers while we awaited the results. I immediately left the doctor's office, drove directly to the pharmacy, and purchased the medicine the doctor prescribed for me; just like anyone would do. I dropped off the script and waited for my medicine. I didn't know much about painkillers and muscle relaxers then, but I quickly learned they not only made my back feel better, but also my entire body and mind.

When I began to take the medications, I followed the doctors' orders specifically. I waited the proper amount of time between doses and didn't mix alcohol with them; at first. As the days passed, I was taking them every 6 hours so my body was building up a tolerance. I wasn't receiving the same numbing affect physically or mentally anymore. This is when I decided to mix the medication with alcohol. This was not a smart move. I took the recommended dose of painkillers and muscle relaxers, then washed it down with a glass of straight liquor. When this combination hit me, I once again felt the numbness I was craving. Then, sadly enough, I just stared into space until I fell asleep.

My wife was watching all this unfold. She had to feel so helpless. I continued this practice on many of my days off. I didn't do it every day at first, but as time passed, I started to dive deeper and deeper with the prescription drugs and alcohol. This occurred simultaneously with my fighting career in mixed martial arts, commonly known as MMA. This is a multi-discipline combat sport including boxing, wrestling, jiu-jitsu, judo, karate, Muay Thai kickboxing, and a host of other fighting techniques. I would release my anger all day training as a fighter, then at night I would medicate and drink myself to sleep. Some morning's my wife would have to shake me intensely to wake me up. I lived this way periodically for almost four years. I'm not proud of this time in my life but it's a part of my fall that needs to be told.

Why did I turn to these substances? I have no idea. I'm very particular about what I put in my body. To this day, I measure almost all my meals to ensure I know how many grams of carbohydrates, fats, and protein I take in. For me to turn to a chemical for help was not like me. I never did this before. My parents weren't big drinkers. Even in college, I wasn't a big drinker either.

As most people know, my personally is very intense. When I set my mind to something, it's on. Get out of my way because whatever it is, I'm going to accomplish it. It's all I know. The problem with this intensity is it spilled over into prescription drugs and alcohol. I went from a person who didn't drink, to someone who was washing down painkillers and muscle relaxers with straight liquor. Not a proud moment.

How did all this change? Well, there were multiple factors. Around the same time, I started talking to my counselor, stopped fighting, and began to detox my body. It was like a switch went off internally. I realized I needed to change my behavior or I was going to die. I took so much medication mixed with alcohol that I'm very lucky to be alive. For most people, the amount I ingested probably would have sent them for the long eternal sleep, but for some reason, my body was resilient. I believe it's because the big man upstairs had a plan for me.

Over the next eight months I forcefully detoxed my body. I stopped taking anything synthetic; cold turkey. No alcohol. No painkillers. No muscle relaxers. No aspirin. No coffee. No caffeine. No sleeping medication. Nothing. I didn't ease off anything. I just stopped, and trust me, it wasn't easy. I experienced intense mood swings, increased heart rate, nervousness, anxiety, cold sweats, sleeping problems, lack of focus, and a sensation where I felt like I had bugs crawling under my skin. It was absolutely miserable.

I laid in bed at night trying to sleep, but my body and mind weren't allowing that to happen. My wife knew I was struggling to detox so she tried to help the best she could. At night, when I kept tossing and turning, she continually checked on me. Unfortunately, I just acted like everything was fine so she wouldn't worry. Most nights, I would go sleep on the floor in the living room. I hated waking her up because of my issues so I took a blanket and pillow and laid flat on the floor in hopes this would relax me. Sometimes it worked, but most of the time, it didn't.

What was going through my mind while I was restless most nights? It was a flood of thoughts and emotions from June 18, 2007 all the way to the point where I was at that time. Then I would think about how hard it was going to be to get on the engine the following day when I had no sleep. My mind was playing tricks on me. You see, for almost four years before this I was medicating myself to sleep. Now, I had to let my body figure out how to sleep on its own. Many nights I wanted to just medicate myself again so I could fall asleep; but I didn't. I wasn't going to let it beat me. So, I just kept staring at the ceiling night after night until I broke the cycle. It took eight months.

After those exhausting eight months, it was like a switch went off in my body. I woke up one morning and almost felt normal. I was surprised but I didn't overthink it. Then the next night, I slept a little more. Then the next night, a little more, until finally, I was sleeping through the night. This was in 2012 when I decided to take my career in a different direction to join the training division. I was having a hard time being on a rig. Most people don't know that, but I was struggling to ride the fire truck at that point. I still couldn't get the incident out of my head. I continued to blame myself every day because the more I learned about the modern fire service, the more embarrassed and ashamed of the lack of knowledge I had before June 18, 2007. I was hoping the training division would educate me even more so I could make a difference in my department and in the emergency services profession.

I'm sure many of you reading this has one time or another turned to alcohol or maybe even prescription drugs. I do not recommend this. The chemicals will only mask a problem that will be right in your face when you sober up. To address the issues, we must gain the proper support and help from family, friends, co-workers, and professionals. Alcohol and drugs are not on the list of helpful resources. They'll make the situation even worse. But please remember, it doesn't make us bad people because we may have done this in the past. It makes us human and anyone that believes they've never made a mistake is just plain arrogant. If you're hurting and turning to substances, please get the help you need by telling someone. Anybody. Please. If you don't, you may ingest a large amount of chemicals mixed with alcohol and not wake up one day. This is not what your family wants. They want you to get help.

CHAPTER

7

The Power of Spousal Support

I didn't understand the power of spousal support and
how much it could've helped not only me after the incident but also my wife. I was so consumed with my own
pain and anger, I was ignoring her feelings. She was hav
ing a difficult time too. I didn't even consider how she
felt. What a jerk I was. Our relationship was struggling
because I closed off myself and all my emotions. I didn't
want her to see me hurting so I put up a wall that grew
taller and taller. She was trying to support me with what
I was going through but as I said earlier, I thought I was

tough and could fix it on my own. This was the worst action possible.

At first, I could tell she didn't know what to do. She would let me try to figure out my issues, then she would attempt to help me. The problem was I would get so upset when she did, eventually she stopped trying and we started to grow apart. Her living her life and me living mine. We still saw each other daily and lived in the same home but it was like we were roommates, not husband and wife. I would work my 24-hour shift, then go train MMA most of the day while she was at her job. When I would come home, she would already be there. We didn't embrace each other when we met after days of being apart. We didn't eat together, we didn't talk much, and we were basically numb. Thinking back on it now it's so sad because we had such a special love when we first met and up to that fateful day in 2007. Then, because I didn't know I needed to ask for help, I ruined it.

Eventually, she started to help me again and believed I would come back to being the man she married. Unfortunately, I would go out all hours of the night and drink. On one occasion, specifically, I went to a local bar to blow off some steam and to forget what kept reoccurring in my mind. I sat at the bar by myself drinking until I was numb. The only information my wife knew was that

I wasn't home. I'm sure she was worried because she'd already saved me numerous times in situations I placed myself in due to my struggles. So, what did she do? She drove to the bars she knew I liked. She wasn't standing for my shenanigans anymore. Suddenly, as I was sitting at the bar, my wife sits down next to me with this stern look and a little smirk. That look made me realize she was in it for the long haul. I couldn't believe she was there. She absolutely hates bars and alcohol. She knows the devastation it does to people from past experiences before I met her and then with my issues. When I saw her, I was happy, and I was sad. I was happy because she was there with me but I was sad because I knew I was disappointing her. When she met me in 2001 I was a man that couldn't be bothered mentally or physically by anything. On that night in 2010, I was broken.

During all this time from 2007 until 2011, I competed in MMA. I turned to this sport immediately after the fire because I needed an avenue to release my anger. As soon as I began fighting, I enjoyed it because I could release my anger to the point where I was exhausted. I had two training partners who liked to train extremely hard and a little unorthodox. We would do bare knuckle jiu-jitsu, punch each other in the face and stomach to build up tolerance, leg kick each other until we could barely walk out of the cage, and then do weights until we vomited. I trained so much my wife would wake me up some nights because I was on my back, in bed, asleep, shadowboxing. I guess when you practice a sport as much as I did, your body takes over. That was actually rather funny. When she woke me up, we started to laugh. It felt so good to be happy together for a change. To this day, I don't believe my wife liked me getting into a cage and physically harming another person, but she understood I needed to release my anger. So, she let it ride. What can I say? She's an unbelievable woman. I'm very lucky she's my wife.

While all this was unfolding, we were also dealing with an incident that occurred at our first home in October of 2008. I went to the MMA gym for a sparring session with my training partners around 6:00 pm. It was raining extremely hard all day but I didn't think anything of it. I thought it was just a rain storm that would eventually pass.

I met up with my teammates at the gym, we embraced each other, and then we warmed up. We did a few minutes of stretching, shadow boxing, jump rope, and finally worked on the punching bag. Once we felt primed, we started our hour long sparring session broken into five minute rounds. During that hour, I was focused on training. No distractions. No phones. No conversation. Just sparring.

Well, when we finished around 8:00 pm, I packed my sweaty gear and stumbled to my car to go home. Before I left, I grabbed my phone to text my wife. When I looked at my phone, I had over 30 missed calls from her. I was now very scared. My wife never called me that many times. If I didn't answer at any time in our relationship the previous seven years, she would just leave a message. She never called repeatedly. Something didn't feel right.

So, with nausea swirling in my stomach and my heart pounding in my chest, I hit redial. I think I actually held my breath while it rang. She answered the phone crying and trying to talk simultaneously. I couldn't understand anything she was saying. Finally, I made out one of the words. I heard "flooded." When I heard that I yelled, "What flooded? Tell me!" She screamed back, "Our house!" Then dead silence. Now we were both crying. "How bad is it?" I asked not really wanting to know the answer.

She then explained to me she watching TV and suddenly the carpet started to bubble in the middle of the living room. She jumped up and ran to look at the neighborhood pond. The water was now less than a foot away from the back door of our house. When she walked back inside moments later, there was a waterfall coming in over all the baseboards. She sprinted upstairs to grab towels thinking she could stop the water. When she ran back downstairs, there was almost two feet of water in the house. She was petrified.

She then called my parents for help because she didn't know what to do. She couldn't get the front door open due to the water pressure. She also had to figure out how to get our 150 pound Great Dane out of the house. At the time my parents had a very large SUV, so they drove down the flooded street through about three feet of water to get to our house. When they arrived, my dad was able to force the door open so my wife and our Great Dane could escape. They then went to my parents' house to wait for me to finish my sparring session.

Once I heard the story of what happened, I decided to drive to the house to investigate how bad it was and to identify if I could salvage any of our belongings. When I approached the front of the neighborhood I saw emergency crews everywhere. However, none of them were down in the flood waters. So, I donned my firefighting pants and waded over a ¼ of a mile to our house.

The water was cold, murky, and smelled of sewage. I was being hit in the legs with objects in the water, so thankfully, I had my firefighting pants on. When I finally made it to our front door, the water was over the door handle. I attempted to open the door, but I couldn't. To say it nicely, I was upset. I started yelling and then kicked the door in with a few strikes of my boot. The door opened just enough where I could then force it with my shoulder. I squeezed through the opening and immediately saw all our belongings floating. Our furniture, our refrigerator, our food, our pictures, our washer and dryer, our photo albums, everything. All our belongings and our home was destroyed. Worse, we had NO flood insurance. None. I stood in the kitchen and looked around at our ravaged home. I couldn't believe what was happening. I felt like the world was closing in on me. I didn't know what I was going to do now.

As a side note, after I learned swift water rescue in 2012, I realized my actions at my home were very unsafe and careless. I could have fallen in a storm drain or worse been swept away. I was lucky that night.

Over the next six months my wife and I lived at my parents' house while we figured out how to fix ours. I started to work overtime shifts so I could replace everything we lost and to rebuild the home. Now, not only were we dealing with my struggles from the fire, we lost everything. Thankfully, we were given aid from local builders to offset the construction on our home. Our house was the worst home that flooded in the area so it would take almost a year for us to be home again. Worse, after we returned home, the house flooded three more times over the next few years. We moved to the second story of the home permanently while we proceeded through litigation. What a nightmare.

While our home was being rebuilt, I continued to fight. However, I started to feel a switch in my emotions when I competed. You see, when I began fighting, I would come out the first round and throw punches until I couldn't lift my arms. This isn't a smart plan as a fighter. In my first competitive fight, I utilized this game plan and was choked so bad I went unconscious. I came out at the bell, started throwing punches, picked the guy up, and slammed him on the mat. I was totally out of control. Then the adrenaline wore off and I was done. He moved to my back and put me in a rear naked choke. I felt the lights going out but I wasn't going to tap. I kept struggling to get out of the choke but then, sleepy time. My opponent choked me unconscious. The next thing I remember, my buddy was waking me up in the ring. I asked him, "Did I win?" He chuckled and said, "No bro, you got choked out." I couldn't believe it. This is when I realized I couldn't fight angry.

After this fight I continued to train hard and finally

learned anger was the enemy. It zapped you of your energy and abilities. I started to also realize when I carried my anger around with me all day, it stole my positive attitude and love for life I once had. With this realization, I continued to fight and improved my record to 3-1. I was progressing quickly and was offered an opportunity to fight Ultimate Fighting Championship (UFC) veteran Houston "The Assassin" Alexander. What an opportunity. If I could beat him, I would move on to the next level for sure. I trained my heart out for the fight but I lost in a decision; which is up for discussion. :)

The day after the fight, I had weird feelings about my life's direction. I was questioning why I was fighting and the road I traveled over the previous four years. Even worse, my eyes were completely swollen shut from the punches that rained down on my face the night before. I was in complete darkness. Lost.

The positive? This is when my wife and I started again. She cared for me over the next three days because I couldn't see anything. She took me to the bathroom, brought me food, and finally decided we needed to go to the hospital due to the tremendous amount of blood pooling in my face. We arrived at the hospital and I was immediately administered numerous tests. The doctor was worried I broke my orbital socket, again. Thankfully, the tests came back negative. However, the doctor told me I had a severe concussion. I already knew that. I think I had a severe concussion for the four years I fought because I was always taking a beating. He then told me to take a few months off to let my face heal. I laughed, but I knew in my mind I needed to stop fighting to get my life together.

My wife was there to take me home and nurse me back to health. While she was doing this, I realized I destroyed our special love. Right then, I decided to change. I began to detox my body from the alcohol, pain-killers, and muscle relaxers I was taking to numb myself. It took eight months for me to feel like myself again. I had severe withdraws where I was sweating profusely all day, I couldn't sleep, my heart was racing, I couldn't hold a thought together, and I was genuinely lost. However, I knew I had to go through this to find my way. Thankfully, my wife was strong enough and did not take the easy way out like many spouses do today. Think back to your vows, "To have and to hold from this day forward, for better or for worse, for richer or for poorer, in sickness and in health, until death do us part." Those words only mean something if you live by them.

One of the main reasons I'm alive to write this today is because my wife Melissa did live by those vows. She took the road less traveled and supported me through all the craziness I put her through. No matter what I did, she was always there for me. Remember the smirk I told you she had at the bar that one night? She had that look on her face because she was showing me she was in it to win it. She wasn't going to yell at me because of what I was doing. All that would have done is upset me and make the situation worse. She had patience, she empathized with what I was going through, and she didn't care about herself. She was more concerned with us getting back to the love we once had. How did she do that? She sacrificed on activities she liked to do and dedicated herself 100% to us.

At that point in her life, she was an IFBB (International Federation of BodyBuilders) professional figure athlete who would travel the country competing as a fitness model. She was incredibly gifted as an athlete so it didn't take her long to excel at this sport. Well, when we started to work on our love, she quit just so she could dedicate herself 100% to our family. She just stopped.

My wife then introduced me to the church. I was skeptical at first but she finally talked me into going. The first service I attended, I sat in this old wooden pew listening to the preacher tell stories of redemption. I would fade in and out of his sermon. My mind just kept wondering. I think my wife recognized this so she would occasionally grab my hand to help me regain my attention. Then I would look at her and she would just smile. That made my heart skip a beat because she cared for me so much. Unfortunately, I didn't know how to do the same. . . yet.

Over the next year, we continued to attend church and spend more quality time together. We were cooking dinner as one, going out to eat, walking around stores, going to play video games, attending sporting events, and finally, living life. This all may seem normal to you, but for someone suffering after a traumatic event, these activities were hard to do. I don't know why. I just know they were. However, my wife broke down those walls so I could start being myself again.

Moral of the story is this: your spouse needs you and vice versa. If you shut out the person you're supposed to love, cherish, and support, your marriage is going to hit some large bumps in the road. But, if you remember you're in this life together, "Until death do us part," you can get through anything; together. Fighting, arguing, and being in competition with each other isn't going to solve anything. It'll make the situation worse. You both must be willing to put the egos down, reflect to when you first met each other, and remember how special the love was. Talk about those times and what steps you both need to take to get back to that special love. Then, you must work on it, together, every single day. It's going to be very challenging. You will cry, laugh, hate yourself at times, cry again, laugh some more, but all the while you're growing closer to each other and having a better understanding of what the other person is experiencing. This is how a relationship grows. I don't know this from reading it in a book. I know this because of what my wife and I experienced and overcame; together. She is the love of my life and I'm very blessed she chose to spend her life with me. I thank the lord every day he allowed us to figure out our love.

Are we perfect? No. We just understand each other deeply and know what the other person needs at certain times. That doesn't come from wasting time on social media looking at what other people are doing. That comes from dedicating our lives to each other to not only have a great marriage, but to help other couples overcome their challenges as well.

These days, when I get on the fire truck or speak at an organization about our story, I always find little love notes in my bags. My wife continually writes these notes to make me smile. They have sweet messages that remind me of how much she loves me and that she's there for me no matter what. That's true love and commitment.

CHAPTER
8

The Importance of Family Support

Throughout the journey you've been reading, I didn't reach out for support from my mom and dad because I didn't want them to worry about me. My parents were absolutely perfect when I was growing up. They always set a good example for me. They never used profanities, drank alcohol, went out partying with friends, or any behavior that could be viewed as bad. I often believed my parents were saints. Their relationship was so strong and all they wanted to do was make the family happy. In a time when most families didn't sit down to eat dinner together because everyone had different activities going on in their lives, my mom and dad made sure we did. Our family was, and still is, very close. I'm lucky to have experienced that support as a young man growing up. I wish I would've utilized that support when I needed it the most.

My parents had to know I was challenged after the fire. My physical transformation was obvious. I went from clean cut military cadet from The Citadel to a guy with a pink mohawk, sleeve tattoos, and a new hobby of fighting in a cage. I'm sure they noticed my attitude change as well. They probably chalked it up to me figuring out life but I don't think they knew I was struggling in so many areas. I didn't want to disappoint them so I just kept quiet about how I was feeling. I tried to act as if everything was great when I saw them or spoke with them on the phone. At that time, my wife and I lived about 20 minutes from their house so we saw them frequently. Since I was in college, I've talked to them on the phone almost daily. There were plenty of opportunities for me to say something, but I didn't. There were many times I wanted to, but I was embarrassed about of how I was feeling. I just didn't want them to think I was weak. How stupid of me.

My parents were aware of my MMA career, although

I don't think they cared for it very much. When I began to fight competitively, I wanted my parents to attend. They didn't want to because they couldn't watch their son get hit. This surprised me at first because they went to almost every baseball game I played in little league, high school, college, and professionally. They also came to my body-building meets when I competed in my mid-twenties. They were continuously supportive, but this time, they drew the line. Today, I totally understand why. There's no way my parents wanted to see my alter ego in a cage fighting another person. That wasn't what they dreamed of me doing.

All I had to do at any time during my four-year struggle was ask them for help. I just didn't know how to do it. I was disrespectful to them, didn't spend enough time with them, and grew apart from the family that raised me to be a hard-working, focused, dedicated, passionate, and caring person. I was everything but any of those traits during my struggle. Such an embarrassment.

Why do I tell you this? Well, because no matter what your going through there are individuals who care about you. Yes, this chapter focuses on my parents because that was my support when I was growing up. However, this doesn't have to be about your parents. What I'm trying to get you to see is we forget about other people's feelings when we're chasing our mind around. When we're constantly thinking about calls that bother us we're not present in the relationships which shape our lives. We change our demeanor and stop being the person our loved ones enjoy being around. We're a ghost of our former selves. We use disrespectful tones, are short in conversations, don't think about feelings, and don't spread positivity in our interactions. I'm a perfect example of this. They say misery loves company. When you get to this point, people around you notice it. Some will want to help you but when you bite their head off repeatedly for caring, eventually they're going to move on. However, some will continue to attempt to break down the walls in hopes of making you change. These are the people who really care about you.

Please don't emulate my actions and pretend everything is fine. This just masked the underlying problem as the alcohol and prescriptions drugs did as well. If you continue to cover up the root causes of the issue, you won't be able to get the help you need in a timely manner. Remember, family is forever. It's not worth destroying a relationship due to pride and ego. Let it go and talk to the people who love you. Trust me, you need their help. Even if you don't think you do.

CHAPTER

9

Share What You've Learned

Sharing what you've learned is essential for growth and progress, especially following a traumatic incident. Why? Because there may be others who have never or will ever experience what you did. If the lessons of a traumatic time are not shared, then what did we really learn? It's a difficult step to take, but it must be done. You may even think you want to forget about traumatic incidents or challenging responses you've been a part of so you don't have to relive them repeatedly. For me, it's the opposite. Each day that passes I don't teach lessons learned from June 18, 2007 is a day this type of tragedy could occur again.

Now, relate this to your career. How many responses have you participated in where you saw trauma? How many responses have you been a part of where you made a mistake or saw others make mistakes? Remember, we are all imperfect people. There is nothing wrong with asking someone what they would do different after they made a mistake. There is also nothing wrong with standing in front of your peers to admit you made one. Mistakes will continue to occur due to the complex systems we operate in. If we don't learn from them and prevent future occurrences, we'll continue to see LODD incidents. These incidents then lead to PTSD for the responders. Some of them could already be struggling with PTSD due to a career full of trauma, then they lose one of their brothers or sisters. This is catastrophic for mental health. It's a vicious cycle we must stop.

Learning from traumatic incidents isn't just important for emergency responders. It's important for profitable organizations as well. Why? Because if a traumatic incident occurs regarding a consumer good, then profits will be reduced and stocks will fall. Let's take Johnson and Johnson for example. In 1982, seven people were killed due to ingesting Tylenol contaminated with Cyanide from an outside source. This occurred in a central location in Chicago, Illinois. However, Johnson and Johnson executives removed over $100 million worth of products from the shelves nationwide. They knew this must be done to regain the public's trust. After the products were removed, Johnson and Johnson reengineered the capsules and packaging. Hence, one of the reasons why it's challenging to open medicine today. They learned from what occurred with intense investigations, they made the public aware of the situation, they worked diligently to make their medicine safer, and then, they reintroduced it to the world. They changed the face of their industry due to seven people losing their lives from contaminated Tylenol. So, what did other medicine manufacturers do? They reengineered their products and containers as well. If Johnson and Johnson didn't share what they learned, then other organizations wouldn't have been able to make their medicine safer.

Another great example of sharing learning is BP. On April 20, 2010, the Deepwater Horizon oil rig in the Gulf of Mexico had a catastrophic failure releasing an estimated 210 million gallons of oil. Eleven people were killed, with 17 sustaining injuries. It has cost the company billions and billions of dollars. Following the accident, investigations were completed to identify the root causes of the failure. After the investigations, BP introduced a national television media campaign where their employees reiterated the importance of safety, spoke about new innovative designs, and most importantly, they were sharing what they learned from the accident. This was monumental. BP shared the lessons learned to help prevent future occurrences.

Now, you're probably asking yourself what does this have to do with PTG? Well, these organizations grew from traumatic incidents. Not just one person in the organization, the ENTIRE organization. If an ENTIRE organization can learn from a traumatic incident and continue to be successful, then you can do the same as an individual. More importantly, you can share your learning with co-workers, family, friends, neighbors, and many others.

So, now your next question. What if I never experience a traumatic incident? Well, I hope you don't. But remember, one major incident doesn't necessarily cause PTSD. It's often related to a career full of traumatizing emergency responses. The same goes for these. Identify the responses that give you the most mental anguish and then be willing to share what you've learned. This doesn't mean a mistake was necessarily made on the incident. It just means that it bothered you. If it bothered you, it probably bothered someone else as well. If you share what you've learned with others, then maybe one day when your co-worker responds to a similar incident, they'll be mentally prepared for the outcome, positive or negative. This may also be therapeutic for you. Knowing you're helping others learn from one traumatic incident, a career full of them, or just incidents you were affected by, is the essence of growth. Specifically, Posttraumatic Growth. Once this fire is ignited inside you, you'll be well on your way to Find Your Mission.

CHAPTER

10

Find Your Mission

I don't know what your Mission is going to be, and more than likely, you won't either at first. I didn't. My Mission just took shape from two major steps: positive thought and my belief in helping others. This opened the door for me to share my story and research at a major emergency services conference. I had no idea if anyone would come to the class or if anyone would appreciate the time, effort, energy, emotion, and knowledge I put into it. I decided I had to put myself out there and speak the truth.

As you could imagine, the morning of the first presentation, I was nervous. Not nervous to speak in front of people. I did that countless times as a baseball player. This time was different though. I was speaking on one of the most scrutinized fire service incidents in history. I had to be factual and not opinionated. My goal was to change the hearts and minds of everyone who attended.

Thankfully, my wife joined me for the first class. She was nervous for me as well. As soon as I woke up, I could feel the anxiety bouncing around in my stomach. I knew the only way to quell that sensation was to exercise. Before I went to the gym, I asked my wife if she would iron my pants. She'd been doing that since 2001 so I wasn't worried. I knew she'd take care of them. My plan was to wear the same outfit I met her in at The Citadel in 2001. It encompassed a gray pair of dress pants and a blue blazer with The Citadel crest on it. The outfit brought me good luck in the past so I decided it was appropriate for this occasion. Lord knows we needed some good luck after all we'd been through.

So, off I go to the gym to complete 99 burpees as fast as possible. As soon as I started, my body was pulsating with adrenaline. I was envisioning what I had to say and focusing on The Mission. Once I finished, I rushed back to the hotel room to prepare for the class. At this point, the anxiety was eased. I was all fired up. I slammed opened the hotel door and said, "Sweetheart! It's time! We're changing the fire service today! You ready?"

As I finished this motivational rant, I saw my wife sitting on the couch crying. She had my pants close to her face and all I could see were tears. In a calming voice, I asked, "Sweetheart, what's wrong? I haven't said anything yet." She looked at me with these sad little eyes and choked out the words, "I ironed a hole in your pants." I asked, "You did what?" Again, she choked out the words, "I ironed a hole in your pants." I paused for a moment, took a deep breath, and asked, "Sweetheart, how did you do that?" She gazed at me with rosy cheeks and so innocently muttered, "I don't know what happened. I just did it the way I've always done it." I looked up to the sky, smiled, and whispered, "Really? Right now? Perfect." I couldn't believe it. The main message in my class was we as emergency responders can't do it the way we've always done it in today's modern environment. I knew at this point, I was on a path bigger than me.

Well, I still had to find pants to wear. I made a few phone calls and couldn't find anyone who had an extra pair. No stores were open. It was too early. I began to pace the room wondering what I was going to do. The hole in the pants was in an area where you couldn't just wear them anyways. You get my point.

Anyway, as I was pacing nervously my wife said, "Sweetheart, I have a pair of pants you can borrow." In disbelief, I asked, "What do you mean?" She exclaimed, "I have a pair of khaki dress pants that should fit you! The only problem is they're bell bottoms." I looked at her like she was crazy. "No Way. I'm not wearing those," I said. She pleaded with me, "Just try them on, please. We don't have any other choice right now." Reluctantly, I stormed in the bathroom to don the khaki bell bottoms. As I stepped in them, I noticed pink lace on the inside. Yes, pink lace. I again paused to take a deep breath so I wouldn't implode before even making the presentation.

So, I finally possessed the courage to put on her pants with my shirt, tie, and blazer. I turned, looked in the mirror, and just shook my head. I opened the bathroom door slowly and eased my way out. My wife saw me and yelled, "Sweetheart, they look good! You look metrosexual." I didn't even know what the hell that meant. I just laughed and said, "Well, I guess this is all we have. Let's do this."

We then gathered our computer and handouts to hurry to the classroom. As we were walking past thousands of firefighters, all I could hear in my head were the lyrics to the song *Staying Alive*. I looked like John Travolta at the beginning of the movie *Saturday Night Fever*. I was not feeling the outfit at all.

As I entered the convention center, there were already people gathered around the classroom. Now the nerves were really setting in. People were eyeing me up and down. I thought they were wondering why I was wearing bell bottoms. Well, in actuality, they were sizing me up as an instructor. We all do this before we go to a class but this time it felt a little different. This group looked hardcore so I knew I had to be on my game. So, how did I begin the class that would become my life's work? I simply said, "Good morning, my name is David and I'm wearing my wife's pants." Of course, the class erupted in laughter, which helped ease my nerves. But then, it was time to begin The Mission.

When I gave the presentation in 2013, I had no idea what would happen following it. I just wanted to teach the class once at the conference. Then, the next thing I knew organizations were contacting me to present for them. People were asking me if I had a website for speaking appointments. So, for the next two months I woke up every morning around 0400 to build my website. I had no experience in doing this and trust me, I had no idea what I was doing. But, what I did know is I could work myself to the point of understanding anything I set my mind too. After the website was up and running I was getting so many inquiries to speak I had to bring my wife on board to help organize it all. This was when our Mission became a reality.

Since the Find Your Mission Tour began in 2013, I've spoken at hundreds of organizations in multiple countries, to over 40,000 people. I've been to places I couldn't have imagined. I've driven through blizzards where I could barely see the front of the car. I've driven on roads that were turned into sheets of ice where I had to dodge tractor trailers that were jackknifed everywhere. I've flown a million plus miles, sometimes on planes that only sat 10 people. I've had food poisoning too many times to count. I'm constantly having sinus issues from recirculated air on planes. I've worked 24 hours on the fire truck, flown for 12 hours, then driven for 3 hours to teach a class that was only 2 hours long, only to drive directly back to the airport for 3 hours, to fly for 12 hours, so I could make it on time to my 24-hour shift on the fire truck. I've done airport sprints in a suit more times than I would like to remember. I've taught in countries where I needed a translator to tell the attendees what I was saying. Who would of thought people in other countries would have learned from the Charleston 9? I did.

In 2016, I spent most of my days on the road teaching or at a firehouse working. I was home with my family for less than 90 days. Why do I do this? Who else is going to?

Are you? If I don't do it, the lessons die. If the lessons die, other emergency responders could die as well. I'm not living with that on my conscience.

These are just a few things I have experienced on The Mission. I don't tell you this to brag. I tell you this so you realize when you do Find Your Mission, you better understand it'll be challenging. Nothing great is ever accomplished by taking the easy road. Whatever you Find Your Mission to be, if you dedicate yourself entirely to it and live it each day with all your energy and passion for it, you will find the meaning to PTG. Will you have rough days? Yes, of course. I wake up in hotels all the time and have to remember where I am. That makes me miss home and my family so much more. Even more challenging is reliving the same incident hundreds of times per year. However, it's for the greater good. If the message I present can save one life, then it's been worth it.

During this journey From PTSD to PTG, I've learned a great deal about myself, life, and people. I've also learned the importance of doing something to make things better, rather than criticizing others or complaining. I'm saddened this journey started due to a traumatic incident. But I have two choices: 1. I can quit living, feel sorry for myself, not help anyone, bring hate and discontent on other people, complain about people that are doing something positive; OR 2. I can put my best foot forward, stay positive every day, help others with what I've learned, and continue to change the hearts and minds of responders around the world. The second answer is definitely the most productive one. You can experience this too if you have the courage to go From PTSD to PTG.

Epilogue

It's my hope the information in this book will enable you to develop coping skills and the strength to overcome PTSD with PTG. As I stated in the beginning, I'm not an expert and I don't profess to be one. I'm just a man with a unique skill set due to the direction my life has taken me. I didn't plan to be a part of a significant event in the fire service and then go on to make it my life's work. What else am I supposed to do? Quit? Let the lessons die because it's hard to talk about? Not happening. That's the easy way out. I owe it to those nine firefighters to continue getting on the fire truck with a good attitude and the willingness to learn. Anything less is unacceptable for me. Trust me, I think about walking away from the job and speaking on the incident every day. I'd be lying if I said I didn't. It's hard doing what I do, plain and simple. However, to do something meaningful in life you must put yourself out there and complete whatever Mission you set out on.

Will my Mission ever be complete? I don't know. But what I do know is I will push on with my Mission as long as I am physically and mentally capable. I know I won't be able to do it forever but I will give it all I can, while I can. Yes, there will be people along the way that don't like or understand why I do what I do. That's all right. I don't do it for them. I do it to honor the nine and to educate you on the importance of learning every single day. If you don't, you'll be standing in front of people singing the same song I'm singing. Believe me, the song I sing sucks the life out of me, but on the other side, it breathes life into people who have similar struggles. The hurricane in my brain may never go away, but I know how to ease it thanks to PTG. I truly hope this information will allow you to do the same. God speed. . . .

Pictures

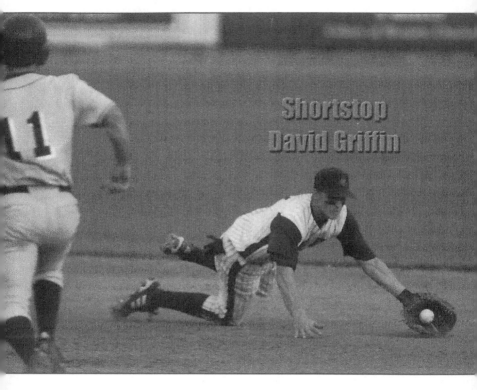

Shortstop
David Griffin

2001 - The Citadel Baseball. Me diving for a ground ball up the middle of the infield during the Southern Conference Tournament where we were crowned conference champions. This was my life before I joined the emergency services profession. Charleston, South Carolina.
Photo courtesy of The Citadel.

2005 – First fire while I was in recruit school. Did salvage and overhaul operations. Charleston, South Carolina.

2008 – Melissa competing in the
International Federation of BodyBuilders
(IFBB) Jacksonville Professional Figure
Contest. Jacksonville, Florida.

2010 – Me competing against Ultimate
Fighting Championship (UFC) fighter
Houston "The Assassin" Alexander In
Charleston, South Carolina. This was my last
fight and when I realized I needed to change
my life.

2012 – Me attending Doctoral Residency Part 1 at Grand Canyon University in Phoenix, Arizona.

2013 – Me nervous before my first presentation in April of 2013 in Indianapolis, Indiana. If you look closely, you can see the khaki bell bottoms I borrowed from my wife because she ironed a hole in my pants before the class.

2013 — Me featured in Oblique Magazine during my time competing in Ironman Triathlons.
2.4-mile swim, 112-mile bike ride, and a marathon 26.2-mile run.This gave me a great
deal of time to reflect on my experiences. It was monumental in my growth process.
Photo Courtesy of Gregg Lambton-Carr.

2013 – Me signing the first copy of *In Honor of The Charleston 9: A Study of Change Following Tragedy* at the release gathering in Charleston, South Carolina.

2014 – Me speaking at The National Fallen Firefighters
Foundation Tampa II Conference in Tampa, Florida.

2014 — Melissa and I spending time together at the Baltimore Orioles game after a speaking engagement in Baltimore, Maryland.

2014 – Me with the Director of The Citadel's Daniel Library, Colonel David Goble, on the day *In Honor of The Charleston 9: A Study of Change Following Tragedy* was enshrined in the rare books room at The Citadel in Charleston, South Carolina. Photo courtesy of Jerry Morrison.

2014 — Me administering the keynote speech at the opening ceremony of Firehouse Expo in Baltimore, Maryland.

2015 – Melissa and I in Laguna Beach, California.

2016 – The Find Your Mission Tour travels to Mexico for its first Spanish presentation.

2016 – Mexican National News broadcast during The Find Your Mission Tour.

2016- Me climbing a mountain in Apache Junction, Arizona.

2016 – Sign at Kenai Peninsula College where I spoke in Soldotna, Alaska.
Thankfully, I didn't see any bears.

2017 – Collage in my locker I look at before I get on the fire truck each shift.
Reminds me of what's important – going home after the tour of duty.

2017 - Melissa and David featured in Oblique Magazine.
Photo courtesy of Editor/Publisher John Di Giovanni.

References

Department of Veterans Affairs National Institute
    for Post-Traumatic Stress Disorder. (2017).
    Retrieved from ptsd.va.gov.

Tull, Matthew. (2017). Rates of PTSD in
    Firefighters. Retrieved from verywell.com.

Made in the USA
Columbia, SC
22 April 2021